ESSENTIAL
CAROL
SINGER

30 carols

SATB

Selected and edited by

BEN PARRY

© 2002 by Faber Music Ltd
First published in 2002 by Faber Music Ltd
3 Queen Square London WC1N 3AU
Amended impression, October 2002
Cover design by Nick Flower
Music processed by Jeanne Fisher
Printed in England by Caligraving Ltd

ISBN 0-571-52512-1

To buy Faber Music publications or to find out about
the full range of titles available please contact your local music retailer
or Faber Music sales enquiries:

Faber Music Limited, Burnt Mill, Elizabeth Way, Harlow, CM20 2HX England
Tel: +44 (0)1279 82 89 82   Fax: +44 (0)1279 82 89 83
sales@fabermusic.com   fabermusic.com

Faber *ff* MUSIC

CONTENTS *first lines* and titles

All tempo, articulation and dynamic markings have been omitted
and are at the discretion of the singers.

Thanks are due to my parents, John and Beate Parry,
and to Phillip and Kathryn at Faber Music for buying the idea!

Ben Parry, June 2002

Angels from the realms of glory

Words: James Montgomery (1771–1854). *Music:* French traditional, arranged by Ben Parry

1. An - gels from the realms of glo - ry, wing your flight o'er all the earth; ye who sang Cre - a - tion's sto - ry now pro - claim Mes - si - ah's birth!
2. Shep - herds in the field a - bi - ding, watch - ing o'er your flocks by night: God with man is now re - si - ding, yon - der shines the In - fant Light.
3. Though an in - fant now we view him, he shall fill his Fa - ther's throne, ga - ther all the na - tions to him; ev - ery knee shall then bow down.

Come and wor - ship Christ the new - born King! Come and wor - ship, wor - ship Christ the new - born King!

Away in a manger

Words: Anonymous, 19th century. *Music:* William J Kirkpatrick (1838–1921), arranged by Ben Parry

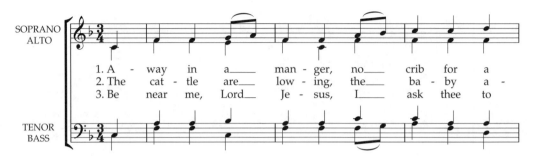

1. A - way in a___ man - ger, no___ crib for a -
2. The cat - tle are___ low - ing, the___ ba - by a -
3. Be near me, Lord___ Je - sus, I___ ask thee to

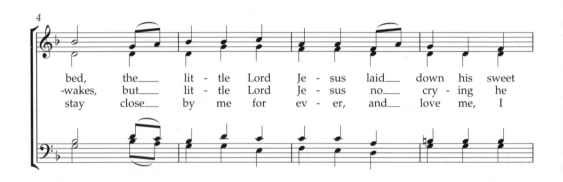

bed, the___ lit - tle Lord Je - sus laid___ down his sweet
-wakes, but___ lit - tle Lord Je - sus no___ cry - ing he
stay close___ by me for ev - er, and___ love me, I

head. The stars in the___ bright sky looked___ down where he
makes. I love thee, Lord___ Je - sus, look___ down from the
pray. Bless all the dear child - ren in___ thy ten - der

lay, the___ lit - tle Lord Je - sus a - sleep on the hay.
sky, and___ stay by my side un - til___ morn - ing is nigh.
care, and___ fit us for hea - ven to___ live with thee there.

Boar's Head Carol

Words and music: English traditional. Refrain: Queen's College, Oxford (1901)

SOLO VOICE
1. The boar's head in hand bear I, be-decked with bays and rose - ma - ry; and I pray you my mas - ters be mer - ry, *quot es - tis in con - vi - vi - o.*

CHORUS
Ca - put a - pri de - fe - ro red - dens lau - des Do - mi - no.

SOLO
2. The boar's head, as I un - der - stand, is the rar - est dish in all the land, which thus be - decked with a gay gar - land; let us *ser - vi - re can - ti - co.*

repeat chorus

SOLO
3. Our ste - ward hath pro - vi - ded this in ho - nour of the King of Bliss, which on this day to be serv - èd is *in re - gi - nen - si a - tri - o.*

repeat chorus

Deck the hall with boughs of holly

Words: Anonymous. Music: Welsh traditional, arranged by Ben Parry

Ding! dong! merrily on high

Words: George Ratcliffe Woodward (1848–1934). *Music:* Thoinot Arbeau (1520–1595), arranged by Charles Wood (1866–1926)

1. Ding! dong! mer-ri-ly on high in heav'n the bells are ring-ing; Ding! dong! ve-ri-ly the sky is riv'n with an-gel sing-ing.
2. E'en so here be-low, be-low, let stee-ple bells be swung-en, and 'i - o, i - o, i - o!' by priest and peo-ple sung-en. Glo - - - - ri - a! Ho-san-na in ex-cel - sis!
3. Pray you, du-ti-ful-ly prime your ma-tin chime, ye ring-ers! May you beau-ti-ful-ly rime your eve-time song, ye sing-ers!

'i-o' pronounced 'ee-o'

8

The first Nowell

Words and music: English traditional, arranged by John Stainer (1840–1901)

God rest you merry, gentlemen

Words: West Country traditional. *Music:* English traditional, arranged by John Stainer (1840–1901)

SOPRANO
ALTO

1. God rest you mer - ry, gen - tle - men, let no - thing you dis -
2. From God our heav'n - ly Fa - ther a bless - èd an - gel
3. Now to the Lord sing prais - es, all you with - in this

TENOR
BASS

-may, for Je - sus Christ, our Sa - viour, was born up - on this
came, and un - to cer - tain shep - herds brought ti - dings of the
place, and with true love and bro - ther - hood each o - ther now em -

day to save us all from Sa - tan's power when we were gone a -
same, how that in Beth - le - hem was born the Son of God by
- brace. This ho - ly tide of Christ - mas all o - thers doth ef -

- stray. O ti - dings of com - fort and joy, com - fort and
name. O ti - dings of com - fort and joy, com - fort and
- face. O ti - dings of com - fort and joy, com - fort and

joy, O ti - dings of com - fort and joy!

© 2002 by Faber Music Ltd.

This music is copyright. Photocopying is ILLEGAL.

Good Christian men, rejoice!

Words: *In dulci jubilo*, English version by John Mason Neale (1818–1866)
Music: *Piae Cantiones* 1582, arranged by John Stainer (1840–1901)

1. Good Christ - ian men, re - joice_____ with heart and soul_ and
2. Good Christ - ian men, re - joice_____ with heart and soul_ and
3. Good Christ - ian men, re - joice_____ with heart and soul_ and

voice!_____ Give ye heed to what we say:
voice!_____ Now ye hear of end - less bliss:
voice!_____ Now ye need not fear the grave:

Je - sus Christ is born to - day! Ox and ass be -
Je - sus Christ was born for this! He hath oped the
Je - sus Christ was born to save! Calls you one and

- fore him bow, and he is in____ a man - ger now:
heav'n - ly door, and man is bless - èd ev - er - more:
calls you all, to gain his ev - er - last - ing hall:

Christ is born to - day!_____ Christ is born to - day!_____
Christ was born for this!_____ Christ was born for this!_____
Christ was born to save!_____ Christ was born to save!_____

Good King Wenceslas

Words: John Mason Neale (1818–1866). *Music: Piae Cantiones 1582,* arranged by John Stainer (1840–1901)

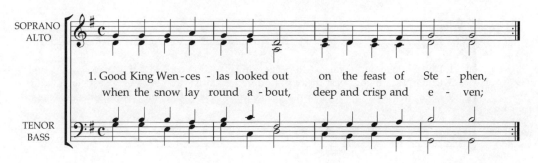

1. Good King Wen-ces-las looked out on the feast of Ste-phen,
when the snow lay round a-bout, deep and crisp and e-ven;

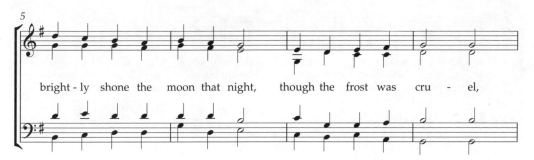

bright-ly shone the moon that night, though the frost was cru-el,

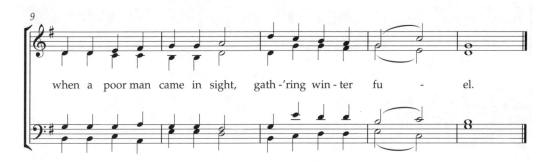

when a poor man came in sight, gath-'ring win-ter fu-el.

2. 'Hither page, and stand by me;
   If thou know'st it, telling –
Yonder peasant, who is he?
   Where and what his dwelling?'
'Sire, he lives a good league hence,
   Underneath the mountain,
Right against the forest fence,
   By Saint Agnes' fountain.'

3. 'Bring me flesh and bring me wine!
   Bring me pine logs hither!
Thou and I will see him dine
   When we bear them thither.'
Page and monarch forth they went,
   Forth they went together,
Through the rude wind's wild lament
   And the bitter weather.

4. 'Sire, the night is darker now,
   And the wind blows stronger;
Fails my heart, I know not how,
   I can go no longer.'
'Mark my footsteps, good my page,
   Tread thou in them boldly:
Thou shalt find the winter's rage
   Freeze thy blood less coldly.'

5. In his master's steps he trod,
   Where the snow lay dinted;
Heat was in the very sod
   Which the saint had printed.
Therefore, Christian men, be sure,
   Wealth or rank possessing,
Ye who now will bless the poor
   Shall yourselves find blessing.

Singers may like to divide the text between upper and lower voices to reflect the narrative.

Hark! the herald angels sing

Words: Charles Wesley (1707–1788) and others. *Music:* Felix Mendelssohn-Bartholdy (1809–1847), adapted

1. Hark! the he - rald an-gels sing,— 'Glo - ry to the new-born King!
2. Christ, by high - est heav'n a - dored, Christ, the ev - er - last-ing Lord:
3. Hail, the heav'n - born Prince of Peace!— Hail the Sun of Right-eous-ness!

Peace on earth and mer-cy mild,—— God and sin - ners re - con - ciled!'
late in time be-hold him come,—— off-spring of a Vir - gin's womb.
Light and life to all he brings,—— ris'n with heal - ing in his wings;

Joy - ful, all ye na - tions rise!— Join the tri - umph of the skies!—
Veiled in flesh the God-head see!— Hail th'in - car - nate De - i - ty,——
mild, he lays his glo - ry by,— born that man no more may die,—

With th'an - ge - lic host pro-claim, Christ is— born in Beth - le - hem:
pleased as man with man to dwell: Je - sus— our Em - man - u - el!
born to raise the sons of earth, born to— give them se - cond birth.

Hark! the he - rald an - gels sing,— 'Glo - ry— to the new-born King!'

Here we come a-wassailing

Words and music: English traditional, arranged by Ben Parry

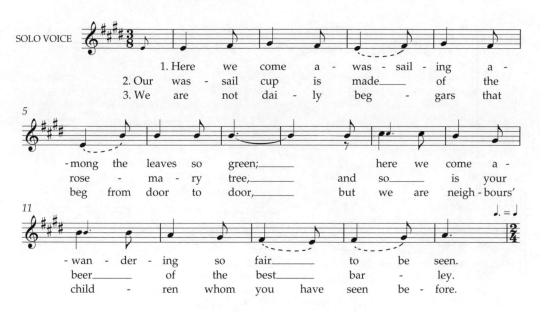

SOLO VOICE

1. Here we come a-was-sail-ing a-
2. Our was-sail cup is made of the
3. We are not dai-ly beg-gars that

-mong the leaves so green; here we come a-
rose-ma-ry tree, and so is your
beg from door to door, but we are neigh-bours'

-wan-der-ing so fair to be seen.
beer of the best bar-ley.
child-ren whom you have seen be-fore.

CHORUS

S.
A.

Love and joy come to you, and to you your was-sail too,_ and God bless you, and

T.
B.

send_ you a hap-py New Year, and God send_ you a hap-py New Year.

4. God bless the master of this house,
   Likewise the mistress too,
   And all the little children
   That round the table go.

5. Good master and good mistress,
   While you're sitting by the fire,
   Pray think of us poor children
   A-wandering in the mire.

The holly and the ivy

Words and music: English traditional, arranged by Ben Parry

SOLO VOICE

1. The hol - ly and the i - vy, when
2. The hol - ly bears a blos - som, as
3. The hol - ly bears a ber - ry, as

they are both full grown, of____ all the trees that are
white as a - ny flower, and____ Ma - ry bore sweet____
red as a - ny blood, and____ Ma - ry bore sweet____

in the wood, the____ hol - ly bears the crown.
Je - sus Christ to____ be our sweet Sa - viour.
Je - sus Christ to____ do poor sin - ners good.

CHORUS

S. A.

The ri - sing of the sun____ and the run - ning of the____ deer,____ the____

T. B.

play - ing of the mer - ry or - gan sweet sing - ing in the choir.

4. The holly bears a bark
   As bitter as any gall,
   And Mary bore sweet Jesus Christ
   For to redeem us all.

5. The holly bears a prickle
   As sharp as any thorn,
   And Mary bore sweet Jesus Christ
   On Christmas Day in the morn.

   repeat first verse in unison

I saw three ships

Words and music: English traditional, arranged by Ben Parry

SOPRANO ALTO

1. I saw three ships come sail - ing in, On

TENOR BASS

Christ - mas Day, on Christ - mas Day, I saw three ships come

sail - ing in On Christ - mas Day in the morn - ing.

* *The verse (in square brackets) may be sung by a solo voice or in harmony.*

2. And what was in those ships all three? *On Christmas Day ...*

3. Our Saviour Christ and his lady, *On Christmas Day ...*

4. Pray, whither sailed those ships all three? *On Christmas Day ...*

5. O they sailed into Bethlehem *On Christmas Day ...*

6. And all the bells on earth shall ring *On Christmas Day ...*

7. And all the angels in heav'n shall sing *On Christmas Day ...*

8. And all the souls on earth shall sing *On Christmas Day ...*

9. Then let us all rejoice amain! *On Christmas Day ...*

In the bleak midwinter

Words: Christina Rossetti (1830–1894). *Music:* Gustav Holst (1874–1934)

Infant holy

Words: Polish traditional, translated by Edith M G Reed (1885–1933), adapted. *Music:* Polish traditional, arranged by Ben Parry

1. In - fant ho - ly, in - fant low - ly, for his bed a
2. Flocks were sleep - ing, shep-herds keep - ing vi - gil till the

cat - tle stall; ox - en low - ing, lit - tle know - ing
morn - ing new; saw the glo - ry, heard the sto - ry,

Christ the babe is Lord of all. Swift - ly wing - ing
ti - dings of a gos - pel true. Thus re - joi - cing,

an - gels sing - ing, No - wells ring - ing, ti - dings bring - ing:
free from sor - row, prais - es voi - cing, greet the mor - row:

Christ the Babe is Lord of all, Christ the Babe is Lord of all.
Christ the Babe was born for you, Christ the Babe was born for you.

It came upon the midnight clear

Words: Edmund Hamilton Sears (1810–1876). *Music:* English traditional, arranged by Arthur Sullivan (1842–1900)

Jingle bells

Words and music: James Pierpont (1822–1893), arranged by Ben Parry

Joy to the world

Words: Isaac Watts (1674–1748). *Music:* W Holford (c1834), arranged by Ben Parry

O Christmas tree

Words: German traditional, translated by John and Beate Parry. *Music:* German traditional, arranged by Ben Parry

This music is copyright. Photocopying is ILLEGAL.

O come, all ye faithful

Words: Anonymous, 18th century, translated by Frederick Oakeley (1802–1880). *Music:* John Francis Wade (1711–1786)

O little town of Bethlehem

Words: Phillips Brooks (1835–1893). *Music:* Collected, adapted & arranged by Ralph Vaughan Williams (1872–1958)

Once in royal David's city

Words: Mrs Cecil Frances Alexander (1823–1895). *Music:* Henry John Gauntlett (1805–1876)

3. And our eyes at last shall see him,
   Through his own redeeming love,
For that child, so dear and gentle,
   Is our Lord in heaven above;
And he leads his children on
To the place where he is gone.

4. Not in that poor, lowly stable
   With the oxen standing by
We shall see him, but in heaven,
   Set at God's right hand on high;
When, like stars, his children, crowned,
All in white shall wait around.

Sans Day Carol

Words and music: English traditional, arranged by Ben Parry

This music is copyright. Photocopying is ILLEGAL.

See, amid the winter's snow

Words: Edward Caswall (1814–1878). *Music:* John Goss (1800–1880)

Silent night

Words: Joseph Mohr (1792–1849), translated by John F Young (1820–1885). Franz Gruber (1787–1863), arranged by Ben Parry

3. Silent night, holy night!
   Son of God, love's pure light,
   Radiant beams thy holy face,
   With the dawn of redeeming grace,
   Jesus, Lord at thy birth,
   Jesus, Lord at thy birth!

Sussex Carol

Words: English traditional, after Bishop Luke Wadding (died 1686). *Music:* English traditional, arranged by Ben Parry

1. On Christ-mas night all Christ-ians sing, to hear the news_ the an-gels bring, on Christ-mas night all Christ-ians sing, to hear the news_ the an-gels bring. News of great joy,_ news of_ great mirth,_ news of_ our mer-ci-ful_ King's birth.
2. Then why should men on earth be so sad, since our Re-deem-er made_ us glad, then why should men on earth be so sad, since our Re-deem-er made us glad when from our sin_ he set_ us free,_ all for_ to gain our li-ber-ty?
3. When sin de-parts be-fore_ his grace, then life and health_ come in_ its place, when sin de-parts be-fore_ his grace, then life and health_ come in its place; an-gels and men_ with joy_ may sing,_ all for_ to see the new-born King.
4. All out of dark-ness we_ have light, which made the an-gels sing_ this night, all out of dark-ness we_ have light, which made the an-gels sing this night: 'Glo-ry to God_ and peace_ to men,_ now and_ for ev-er-more._ A-men'.

Unto us is born a son

Words: *Puer nobis nascitur*, 15th century, translated by Ben Parry. Music: *Piae Cantiones 1582*, arranged by Ben Parry

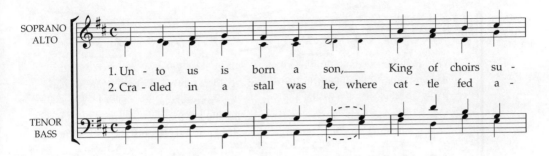

1. Un - to us is born a son,___ King of choirs su -
2. Cra - dled in a stall was he, where cat - tle fed a -

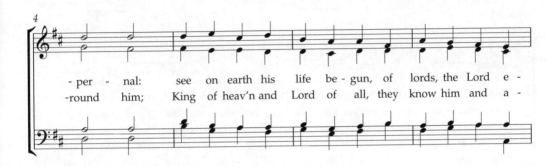

- per - nal: see on earth his life be - gun, of lords, the Lord e -
-round him; King of heav'n and Lord of all, they know him and a -

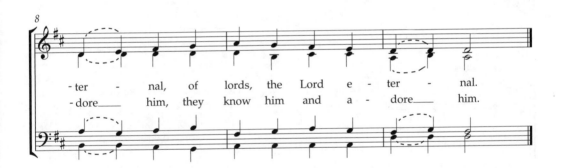

- ter - nal, of lords, the Lord e - ter - nal.
- dore___ him, they know him and a - dore___ him.

3. Of his love and mercy mild,
   Hear the Christmas story:
   O that Mary's gentle son
   Might lead us up to glory,
   Might lead us up to glory.

4. O and A and A and O,
   Cantemus in choro,
   Voice and organ, let us sing
   Benedicamus Domino,
   Benedicamus Domino.

We three kings of Orient are

Words and music: John Henry Hopkins (1820–1891), arranged by Ben Parry

We wish you a merry Christmas

Words and music: English traditional, arranged by Ben Parry

[verses may be sung as a solo or in harmony]

SOPRANO
ALTO

1. We____ wish you a mer - ry Christ - mas, we____
2. Now____ bring us some fig - gy pud - ding, now____
3. For we all like____ fig - gy pud - ding, for we
4. And we won't go un - til we've got some, we____

TENOR
BASS

wish you a mer - ry Christ - mas, we____ wish you a mer - ry
bring us some fig - gy pud - ding, now____ bring us some fig - gy
all like____ fig - gy pud - ding, for we all like____ fig - gy
won't go un - til we've got some, we____ won't go un - til we've

Christ - mas and a hap - py New Year!
pud - ding, and____ bring some out here!
pud - ding, so____ bring some out here!
got some, so____ bring it out here!

CHORUS 9

Good ti - dings we bring to____ you and your kin: we

13

wish you a mer - ry Christ - mas____ and a hap - py New____ Year!

While shepherds watched their flocks

Words: Nahum Tate (1652–1715). Music: Este's Psalter (1592)

1. While shep - herds watched their flocks by night, all
2. 'Fear not,' said he (for might - y dread had
3. 'To you in Da - vid's town this day is

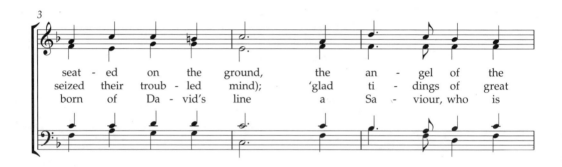

seat - ed on the ground, the an - gel of the
seized their troub - led mind); 'glad ti - dings of great
born of Da - vid's line a Sa - viour, who is

Lord came down, and glo - ry shone a - round.
joy I bring to you and all man - kind.
Christ the Lord; and this shall be the sign:

4. 'The heavenly babe you there shall find
   To human view displayed,
   All meanly wrapped in swathing bands
   And in a manger laid.'

5. Thus spake the seraph; and forthwith
   Appeared a shining throng
   Of angels, praising God, who thus
   Addressed their joyful song.

6. 'All glory be to God on high,
   And to the earth be peace;
   Good will henceforth from heaven to men
   Begin and never cease.'